This is a short book and my hope is to give you a foundation to begin your path to business ownership. For those of you that are totally new to this; I hope to give you a concept and clue about where to start. If you have already started your enterprise; maybe there will be some tips which you may be able to use along the way. Remember this is a general tour through the world of starting an enterprise. As they say, everybody has to start somewhere. So let's start at the beginning.

ISBN-13:
978-1489596888

ISBN-10: 1489596887
Your book has been assigned a CreateSpace ISBN.

Chapter 1	*How Do You Eat an Elephant?*
Chapter 2	*Money is Not a Motivator*
Chapter 3	*Which Business Should You Start?*
Chapter 4	*Don't Be a Know it All.*
Chapter 5	*Do You Have What it Takes?*
Chapter 6	*How To Get From Here to There?*
Chapter 7	*Create an Elephant Eating Plan*
Chapter 8	*Wear Your Colors Everywhere You Go*
Chapter 9	*Time is Money*

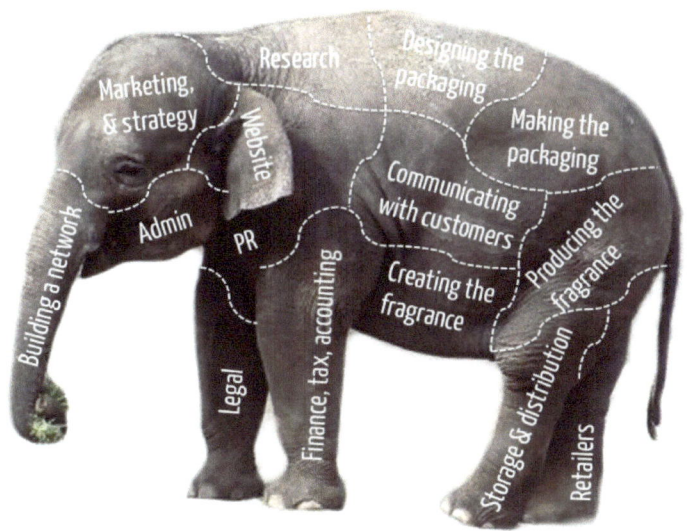

How Do You Eat an Elephant?

One Bite at a Time.

Eating the Elephant

According to the November 2009, labor statistics report by the Bureau of Labor, 7% of all working Americans want to be self-employed. That means there are at least 10 million others who are trying to reach the target called self-employment. So if you are reading this book, you are not alone. What sets you apart is the fact that you have taken the first step towards self-employment. I recently saw an article that stated that there are only three things that intrinsically motivate us:

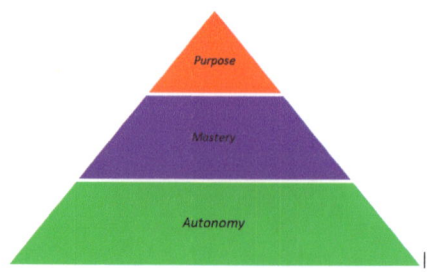

A Purpose Driven business:

Hopefully, this business is something you would do even if you never received a dime. If it is, you are sure to have a passion which drives the purpose which pushes your mastery of the skills necessary to become solely responsible for your success. I just said a mouth full. Try saying that five times non-stop.

The motivation for success begins with purpose, mastery and autonomy and it is this process which drives us to succeed.

Lifes purpose is what fuels our passions.

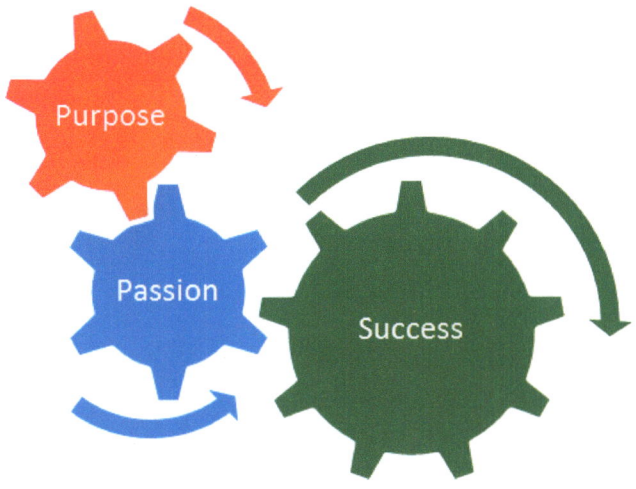

So ask yourself, will my business fuel my passion to stay motivated to be successful?

What is my purpose? Why do I want to have this business?

Keep in mind, money is not a Motivator.

What I mean is: You should love your business to the point that it is your purpose in life. You should be willing to work on it autonomously (using your business plan). And you must, must become a master at it.

I am sure that you have heard the saying;

 Do what you love and the money will follow. It's true. And you will have even better results if it helps others. That's the intrinsic value of it. So before you start; take a look at your reasons for starting this business.

It is the helping of others that will push each step on the path to success.

Once upon a time, years ago, in a land far, far away, where the grass was greener than green and there were more trees than you have ever seen, there lived a little boy whose father was a shoemaker and whose mother was baker.

Every other child whose parents were makers and bakers always followed in their parents footsteps and became makers of some type.

Yet this little one did not want be a maker or even a baker.

This little one only dreamed of magic.

He even thought that the grass and the trees were magic....

The magic in the grass and the trees drew the little one to the meadows. They filled his mind with a belief that magic was possible even doable.

It was the magic that motivated him to finish his chores early just so he could go to the meadows.

Chapter 2 - Money is Not a Motivator

Many of you believe that it is the money that will motivate you. I am here to tell you that you are wrong. Study after study has shown that money only motivates physical activities. Running your business is a cerebral activity. There is an enormous amount of thinking, planning, strategizing and development involved. And you have to love it. It needs to have a purpose, something that drives you work on it and to master it.

Right now you are motivated to start your business. You have purchased this book and you are on a path of discovery. But after the newness wears off, after the novelty is over and the grind of everyday sets in: How will you stay motivated? Can you create ways to reward yourself so that you can maintain your motivation and momentum towards success?

Receiving and planning for rewards to maintain the motivation. So **What's Your Motivation?**

Motivation to keep going is critical. So don't forget to reward yourself along the way. Spend some time learning what your pay date is. For some of us, our pay date is the ability to spend money on things other than bills and mortgage payments. For others, it is the freedom to pay for an all-expense vacation for our parents or grandchildren. Whatever your pay date is, it must be something that will drive your determination to continue on the path of business ownership.

WHAT IS YOUR MOTIVATION?

Chapter 3 - Which Business Should You Start?

As you start your business you will need to consider what type of business you are forming. If you are starting some type of service business and you will be the only one providing the services.

There four types of businesses which you can start:

>Limited Liability

>Partnership

>Sole proprietorship

>S or C Corporation

(*see the appendices for explanations of each type*)

You should make an appointment with a trusted professional to discuss the advantages and/or disadvantages of each type of entity. Let me emphasize, as a business owner it is in your best interest to hire professionals to help you in these areas. You would not try to perform major reconstructive surgery on yourself and you should not do so on your business. Trust the experts to do what they do best, so you can concentrate on the rest.

Chapter 4—Don't Be a Know it All

Financing

Once you have completed your business plan you can contact your local banker, however remember banks are in the business of making money; so if you can't show them how the bank will make money by lending you money they won't approve the loan. A business plan shows the bank you are serious; so do your homework. Owning a business is not for the faint of heart. It takes time, energy and commitment to go the distance.

In your area, there is sure to be a local SCORE office. SCORE is a small business counseling center run by the federal government to provide start-up and growth counseling and assistance to small businesses. You can also find them on-line at www.score.org.

Many people utilize their savings, credit cards and OPP (other people's money) to start their business. If you have friends, family and other relatives who you can tap into for additional funds, do so. But remember these are loans and they must be repaid. The good news is they are also a business expense and therefore are tax deductible. So don't forget to document the loan and report them to your accountant.

Licensing

In most cities, you are required to secure a license to do business and for some of you there may also be additional state licensing requirements. I suggest you check with the local city hall to obtain the license. Regardless of what type of business, the license authorizes you to conduct business in the city where you are conducting business. If you are working from home or will rent or purchase office space; licensing is required. Don't skip this step as there are penalties for none payment. For the state license, you will need to contact both Department of Revenue which collects and authorizes sales taxes as well as the Department of Professional ***Registration.***

Once you have chosen what type of company you will form, you will also need to register the business with the county or the state in which you live. If you chose to do a sole proprietorship, you will need to register as a DBA(doing business as). This requires that you

Advertise in the local newspaper for a period of 3 weeks and complete the necessary documents which will register your business in the county. If you chose to incorporate as either an S or C corporation; the registration is completed with the Secretary of State. Again, remember to contact you accountant for the proper procedure and entity which you incorporate under.

Taxes

And finally, you must register your business with the Internal Revenue Service. This means you must apply for and receive a FEIN (Federal Employer Identification Number). Regardless of whether you initially hire employees or not, this number is used to track your federal tax payments.

Apply for your FEIN at:

http://www.irs.gov/businesses/small/article/0,,id=102767,00.html.

It is free and sometimes can be received the same day. The federal government requires that you pay taxes on any income which you receive on a quarterly basis; therefore be sure to submit a minimum of 15% of your income to them each month. Once you receive the FEIN number, the IRS will send payment booklets to receive the quarterly payments.

I suggest the minimum of 15% of your income to be sent on a quarterly basis to ensure that you don't have a huge tax bill at the end of the year. *(This is for those of you who can't or won't contact an accountant right away)*

But remember, you need to consult your accountant for the appropriate amounts which must be given to the IRS. The 15% rule is just a rule of thumb to ensure that you begin the habit of paying taxes. Many a small business owner has gone under because of back taxes.

Taxes are the price you pay for having your own business. Profits are the rewards you get you having your own business. You can't truly have one without the other. So take the bitter pill and remember if you have to give the government 50% of the money you made this year, it's still 50% more than you had before you started your business.

Insurance

There are three types of liability coverage that any business owner can purchase.

General Liability: this is a protection against your negligence. If you forget to repair a tile in your ceiling and one falls on my head, you are liable. General liability says that everyone must be a prudent person. Take care of your property such that it does not harm others.

Professional Liability: Dependent upon your location, you may be required to purchase insurance to protect against an act of malpractice. This ensures that if a client wishes to sue you do to a perceive misdeed or misconduct on your part, the insurance will protect against any awarded damages. Professional liability is must if you starting a service business.

Product Liability: This type of insurance protects against harm done to your customers due to product defects. It does not protect in the case of a customer who misused the product; however in either case the damage must be proven in court. If you are designing a product, you should discuss this type of insurance in detail with your insurance agent.

My biggest caution to you in this area; hire experts. Do not attempt to assume that you know what type of insurance you need. Do the research, contact professionals and be sure to ask questions. A mistake at this juncture can be extremely costly later.

Remember you are not the first to start a business so be willing to ask yourself questions about your own expertise and where you will need to hire others to help. Take the time to look for potential deal breakers: things that kill the deal for you.

Please Don't Kill Your Business Before it Even Starts.

There are things that are fatal to small business; for example here are some business mortality makers:

1. The owner's unwillingness to hire experts to do the work.(frugality)
2. The owner's inability to let employees do their jobs (micro-management)
3. The owner's inability to when to work in the business and when to work on the business. (Letting go so you can grow)
4. The owner's forgetting to maintain receipts for expenses. (causes tax problems)
5. The owner's lack of management and leadership. (Does not review business plan for guidance, direction and adjustment. Remember the plan is like your compass, it can tell you which direction you are going and where you may need a course correction.

Before you hand yourself the keys to your new home office

Ask yourself the hard questions:

- Do you really want to operate independently and be the person making all the decisions and shouldering all the responsibility?

- Are you willing to work hard and make the sacrifices starting a small business entails?
- Do you have the self-confidence and self-discipline that will enable you to persevere and build your new enterprise into a success?
- How good are you at honoring your commitments to yourself and to others?

If you have answered "no" to any of these, you're probably not

ready .Don't believe the hype, overnight success stories are just that... stories. The truth is that most people dream of success…Successful people wake up in the morning and work really hard at it day after night after day. If you answered all three of these basic questions yes, then you're ready to think seriously about starting a small business. But remember not everyone who is thinking of starting a small business should run a business; the real question is how much do you want it?

What do you believe you can do?

Every day the little one would run to the grass fields after school and fall down in the plush greener than green grassy meadow, surrounded by the fresh smells of golden daffodils and lilies. The colors yellow and white floated all around him, blew in the wind and comforted him as he lay imaging his future. Though he did not know what magic was he knew he believed in it. He could feel the magic all around him and when he closed his eyes the magic was there. The little one was certain to his core that this what he wanted for his future. Days would pass with the sun rising high into the sky and the little one would lie there wondering how he could be a magician. Even though he did not really know what a magician did. One afternoon as the little one ran as fast as he could through the greener than green grass; he chased the sun's path until he could not run any further so finally he lay down and allowed the grass blanket to surround him. It covered him until he was totally invisible in the meadow and the bright blue endless sky seemed to connect to his outstretched hand as voice spoke softly from with one of the floating puffy white clouds "You are here" the low and willowy voice rolled down. The little one looked up at the cloud and boldly replied, "I knew you would come". And the cloud responded tersely, "If you knew I would come, why did you not call me before?"

And the little one replied, "Because I was not ready".

"Ready? Asked the cloud,

"Ready, for what?"

21

This is a story about belief; both commonly held and individual.

Ask yourself….

Whose value system are you holding onto?

What do you value?

Each person is unique

Everyone makes the best choices available to them at the time they make them.

There is no failure, only feedback

The person with the most flexible thinking and behavior has the best chance of succeeding.

Knowledge, thought, memory and imagination are the result of sequences of ways of filtering and storing information.

(Drawn from NLP at Work by Sue Knight)

Do You Have What it takes?

Don't lie to yourself...

This business will cost time and money.

What do you really believe it takes to run a successful business?

Most of you, will like me, start your business from home. Working from home, before, during and after work, between coffee breaks, at 2:00 in the morning and on weekends and maybe even holidays is the life of a small business owner. It is a serious commitment.

It requires time. Time is our biggest and most precious resource. Why because it is limited. Time has limitations which you put upon yourself and others place upon you. You may think you have all the time in the world, but the real truth is you don't. You are committed to so many other things even before you decide to start a business, especially if you have a full-time job. Time becomes a precious commodity which you must allot effectively to be successful. And, unless you are going to work on this business full-time you will simply have to give up some of your other activities to start and run your business. But if you really want it and are willing to commit to it, there is nothing like it. If you are ready and really want to own the show.

Finally if you made the hard decision,

Be proud of yourself.

Many are called, a lot will answer, some will follow through, a few will stay the course and those that do will succeed with a little luck, a lot of sweat, perseverance and a plan. Soooo, if you are ready …Here we go, it's going to go fast.

So grab hold and hold on and next year this time you will have been in business for a year.

I commend you for making the commitment to take the road less traveled.

Chapter 7 *Create an Elephant Eating Plan*

As you begin this journey to business ownership, I want you to really get to know you, as a business owner. You can create yourself in the image of any one. Think of who you would like to pattern your business after. What successful person would you like to emulate? When you choose the person or business which you will model, let it help you to create both patterns of behavior as well as measurements of success and excellence in your business. Having a pattern of business will help you to pattern your success and create a consistent performance level.

As you are create your business plan; take time to observe other business leaders who are performing in the manner and at the level to which you aspire. If possible, observe and listen to these business models in action. Attend Chamber of Commerce and business meetings so that you can not only build rapport with the model but also interview, watch and listen to what they have to offer. Pay close attention to their movements, their language and word cues. Model their behaviors both verbal and non-verbal as you refine your own methods of doing business.

Business ownership can be a chance for growth and discovery as well as life changing but only if you have a clear plan and road towards your future success. In order to follow the road, you will need a road map. For business owners; that map is called a Business Plan. Your business plan will be your guide through on this journey; you must hold on to it; consult it; much like you would a compass and adjust directions when you found that you have gotten off course.

The name of your company will become an integral part of your business plan. It is part of the strategy to develop your corporate identity. Take a look at the logos below: how many of them cause an automatic picture or commercial to come to mind. So choose your logo and name wisely.

STEP ONE

Choose a name. This is important. It must be something that people can remember. Take for instance the name *"The Business Doctor"*. What thoughts come to top of mind? Your business name is your calling card. It's the leave behind in their brain. Even if they don't remember your name, you want them to remember the business name. Don't choose something that is close to a competitor's name. Once you have chosen the name contact your accountant to decide whether register it as either a DBA or corporation.

You might not believe that a name can make or break a company, but how many of us own an Edsel?

Released too much fanfare in 1957, this car of the future was discontinued less than 2 years later in 1959.

STEP TWO

You need a road map. That is your business plan. It must be flexible in the early stages, so don't get

frustrated if you have to revise it along the way. The business is the road map and compass you will use to measure your distance to your destination. Think of starting your business as a journey to Success land. As with any trip you need a destination and a map of sites and locals along the way. Since this trip is on the road less traveled, landmarks, mile markers and locations to stop for refueling needs to planned so that you don't veer off course and end up in the Unemployment City or worse yet Bankrupt City.

Create your business plan that answers these questions:

1. What Type of business?

2. How will I do business

3. Who will I sell too?

4. Where will I sell?

5. What is different or the same about my product/service as my competition?

6. What methods will I use to sell my products/services?

7. What additional tools, equipment, training do I need to be successful?

8. How much money do I have available to run my business?

9. Where am I now in the business market?

10. Where will I be within 3 months, 6 months and 1 year? Create your goals today!(make them measurable; what steps will I take at each milestone? Remember your business plan is your roadmap to success)

11. How much money and sales do I want to make by each of those times? (make it quantifiable: give it a number)

12. What are my standards? What is important to me for myself, for my clients and my employees?

13. How will I introduce myself and my company to my peers, my clients and suppliers?

When the Going Gets Tough: How Will You Survive?

It was early morning as she sat on her green gardening board, tending her garden on the edge of the Maysa desert. Just as the sun slid slowly to the edge of the horizon, she heard the first roar of the motorcycles. The woman looked up as the gang pulled next to her fence; loudly barking that they needed water and fuel.

Slowly the elderly woman rose from her seat moving quietly towards the three men. As she approached them, she noticed that one of them sat a further away and did not speak like the other two constantly commanded her for the supplies.

Softly she spoke, "A day without water in this desert is certain death, is it not?"

Angrily the men gestured for her to fill the outstretched canteen.

"Yet even in the sun one can find shade for the even the lowliest bush cast a shadow".

Still none of the men responded as she rambled on.

"Under every rock the snakes slivers, slowly, methodically across the dry desert. Rocks and hollows are his home, how do they live? Is it due to their thick skin that shields them from sunburn or survival that makes them search under for life giving water?

As she handed the last canteen to the men,

She smiled quietly and said even the snake knows the way home, though the thorns of the cactus plants which feed the antelope prick him as he sucks the water flesh for nourishment in the dry seasons even while is dry flicking tongue flicks back and forth across the salty rocks.

On the sixth day in the desert the lone biker sat quietly watching the night sky....his lips cracked and broken. Softly he heard a quiet voice drift over him as he looked down at the slivering snake and smiled.

Now I know the way…

STEP THREE

Contact your local bank and open a business account. You will need a copy of your incorporation papers or DBA notice which you received from the newspaper and the county. You may have to wait for the papers to return to you so keep moving through the steps.

STEP FOUR

When you completed your business plan, you wrote the goals/milestones which you want to achieve within 30, 60 and 90 days. I like to call this the creating an elephant meal plan.

Question: How do you eat an elephant?

Answer: One bite at a time.

Therefore you must create mini-meal which will help you to eat this huge elephant called your own business.

Have you ever seen an elephant up close? To climb on their backs, the elephant must kneel down and still you would need a step ladder to get on board.

Elephants are massive just like the goals in your business plan.

Look at your 3 month, 6 month and 1 year goals, Today they may seem massive. Huge in comparison to where you are today, right? But just like the elephant, we can make them kneel down to your size and create a step ladder to successfully mounting each step to your goals.

*You must not only believe that you can.
You must know that you can no matter how big the challenge.*

What is the difference between believing and knowing?

The little one looked up at the cloud and boldly answered, "I knew you would come".

And the cloud replied, "If you knew I would come, why did you not call me before?"

And the little one replied, "Because I was not ready".

"Ready? The cloud replied. "Ready, for what?" the fluffy question floated slowly around inside his head.

The little one smiled and slowly stood to his feet. His arms outstretch, hands still touching the sky. "To go", he replied.

"Go, where are you going?"Asked the cloud softly.

"Where you take me…"

And where might that be? , asked the cloud.

"Where the clouds become rain and sunshine.

Where the magic happens, where the rainbow ends, at the pot of gold filled with magic".

And as the cloud floated slowly down to the little one, it asked softly,

"What makes you think that you can go there?"

And little one answered." Because I know I can.

What do you know for certain?

Chapter 6   ***How To Get From Here to There?***

STEP FIVE

Are you ready to go to work on your business?

As you begin step 5: Ask yourself the following questions: This questions will help you create a daily work schedule. *(It is the meal plan for eating this elephant called Starting Your Own Business)*. Begin with these questions: (remember you need to commit to your company).

- What time of the day shall I work and for how long?
- Will you work on it for one hour per day, seven days a week?
- What will you do for each hour that you work on your business?
- Are you willing to work after five o'clock and if so what will you do?

My Daily Business Schedule	**My Daily Work Schedule** Indicate in the space below the times of day you will work on your business. Just like any job you need to know the working hours.						
	Mon	Tue	Wed	Thurs	Fri	Sat	Sun
6 am - 8 am							
Morning							
Lunch							
Afternoon							
Evening/After Work (regular job							
After Dinner							

STEP SIX

Create your identity.

> Go to www.google.com to search your potential website name.
>
> If you decide to create a website for your business, try www.godaddy.com.
>
> Here you can search for your domain name (website name)
>
> As well as create a website for a small fee.

What is the image you want to project to them. Imagine is about branding: Implanting your business in their memory. To do this you will need you will need business cards and stationery. Contact the local office supply store (like Office Depot or Office Max) they will print a small amount of cards for a minimal cost. Or you can go to vistaprint.com to print your first 250 cards for free.

Whichever you use, be consistent.

Chose a color scheme for the company and use it consistently on brochures, flyers, business cards and stationery.

All of these items create your brand.

Wear Your Colors Everywhere You Go

It was the first day of school and the boy did not want to go. He did not know anyone in the new school and felt sad because no one would recognize him. Last month, he and his parents had moved across town to a new neighborhood and all of his old friends now attended a different school.

Nostalgically, he donned his basketball jersey that prominently displayed the DunBar Lions name and colors across his chest. At the last moment he picked up his baseball cap and backpack both sporting the high school mascot and bright colors of orange and black.

On the ride to the school, he imagined how he would tell them he was a lettered basketball player and his teams stats. Goodbye son, his Dad said as he drove the car close to the curb in front of the school. Reluctantly, he climbed from the car and started towards the stairs.

Hey Dunbar, he heard as he mounted the stairs.

Turning his head slightly to the right he saw is schools colors brightly reflected in a baseball wearing kid sitting on the banister.

"I'm new here too.

When did you go to Dunbar? He asked as they both walked into the school.

Chapter 8 *Wear Your Colors Everywhere You Go*
Create your marketing plan.

How will you get the word out to your potential customers? What methods will you use to let them know you are there? For some of you this sounds like selling. And this is frightening. Many of you will say. I hate selling and I hate rejection. How can I market my product, my service and myself?

Simple.

Put yourself in front of other people.

If you want to have a successful business, you have to sell one thing; You. Putting yourself in front of others does one thing only: creates an impression. The impression you make allows your customers or potential sales people to strengthen their belief in you and thereby your product.

And yes, I said potential sales people. Each new contact which you build rapport with can become a sales representative for you.

The more people who you can impress; the more potential representative referrals you will develop.

What should be in your marketing

plan?

Advertising, Sales, Publicity, Research, Planning and Merchandising

The Marketing Plan

Advertising is the mass media you have to pay for to reach the multitude of customers: commercials on radio and television; print ads in magazines and newspapers as well as web/banner ads on the internet. All of these are costly. And unless you have a budget for advertising; require a long-term commitment to see results.

Sales are very personal and can see a quick turn-around if you are consistent and follow through on your commitments. When you make a sales call whether in person or by phone be sure to

follow-through with whatever things you have agreed upon. Good customer service can generate repeat business as well as referral business. Bad customer services, forgotten phone calls and un-kept promises; can tarnish your fragile reputation; causing you to stall out of the starting gate.

Research and planning go hand in hand and can make you look like you know more than you do in an initial presentation. Therefore set that meeting with the client and remember to research them, plan the presentation and practice before you present.

Merchandising *i*s the nuts and bolts of product sales. It is what you use to display your product. Make it pretty: Pretty sells. Lights and shiny displays are still the rage.

 If you don't have a store front and sell out of the trunk of your car; it must still look nice.

Clean display boxes; unwrinkled wrapping paper and clear flat surfaces; will make you customers respect your business as much as you do. The final part of marketing is publicity.

Publicity is what we think of when we think of celebrities. Public relations firms and marketing companies make us feel as if publicity is a part of
nuclear science and not to be understood by the average man. Don't be intimidated by it. Press releases can be written and submitted and if you want to become a local business celebrity; you will get good at it.

Magazines and Newspapers are also places where you will be able to build free publicity so don't overlook them. Contact your local newspaper; discuss writing a column or blog. Write letters to the editor. They are published in both print and on-line. Check newsletters that are related to your field of business and if you can't find one; start-one. Most newsletters are sent via email these days so be sure to collect email addresses as they can become subscribers to your blogs and newsletters.

Chapter 9   *Time is Money*

STEP SEVEN

Review your business plan to see what equipment you are to purchase. Order only the essential equipment like; office supplies, phone, desk, chairs, computers and filing cabinet. Don't be afraid to purchase used office equipment. Lots of pieces are available on-line and from Craig's list. (Remember to keep all your receipts.)

Figure out how much you will charge. Don't forget to calculate your overhead and expenses.

Overhead and Indirect Cost Examples
Secretary
Office Rent/% of home
Telephone (cell & office)
Postage
Personnel benefits
Equipment
Office Supplies
Marketing Cost
Dues and subscriptions
Automotive Payment
Insurance (car, business, professional)
Accounting and legal
Miscellaneous
Total Overhead Costs

(These are examples of some of the charges which can be included in overhead)

If you are in a service business and charge and hourly rate over and above the overhead costs; do your research. Conduct an informal study of the competition. Call around to find out what is the current rate hourly rate. If you set your rate to low, you start out as you mean to go. Set it to high and you may price yourself right out of the market. This is a caveat for all of you who are afraid to tell people how much you charge.

When you go to the grocer:
Does he hesitate to tell you the cost of a head of lettuce?
No!
If you drive into McDonalds or Burger King; their prices are clearly and prominently displayed for the world to see.
Time is Money- so value your own time and charge for it.

Spend some time calculating the actual cost to do business so that you will not hesitate to tell your clients what it will cost them to do business with you.

Many a small business owner has become a statistic simply because they discounted their way out of business; trying to get the business from a client.

Don't roll off the road to Success due to lack of fuel.

Profits are the fuel that feed the business.

Calculate Your Daily Fee

Figure out the total amount of your overhead expenses for one month. Multiple the total times 12 for the annual overhead cost.

To calculate your personal daily labor rate. Determine your annual salary you wish to earn based upon your credentials.

For example annual salary of $50,000 would have a Daily labor rate of $191.50.

$50000 divided by 261 days.
(we have subtracted the 104 Saturdays and Sundays from the 365 days of the year)

Daily Labor Rate plus Overhead Cost = Total Cost

Total Cost x 20 per cent = profit margin

(or whatever you determine your profit margin to be)

Your Daily Fee is calculated as:

Total Cost plus Profit Margin=Daily Rate/Fee

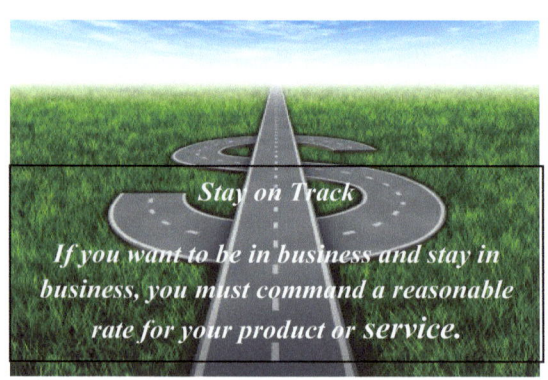

Just because you don't have a lot of profit; does not mean that you have a not-for-profit business!

STEP EIGHT

Look at your Business Plan regularly
(remember to use your road map and compass)

In this step you need to create a list of all possible clients and sources of referrals. If you have ever tried to start a business or been involved in any networking marketing company, they will all suggest that you make a list of all of your friends and family. And while I believe that family can refer business to you, let's not start with them.

However, starting with your business associates and contacts which you have developed through employment, church, school and hobbies is definitely acceptable.

If you do not have any or do not want to contact these people for referrals or business (*you are missing business here*), you will need to create a list of industries and potential clients who would need or use your service/product.

Marketing and Selling Cycle

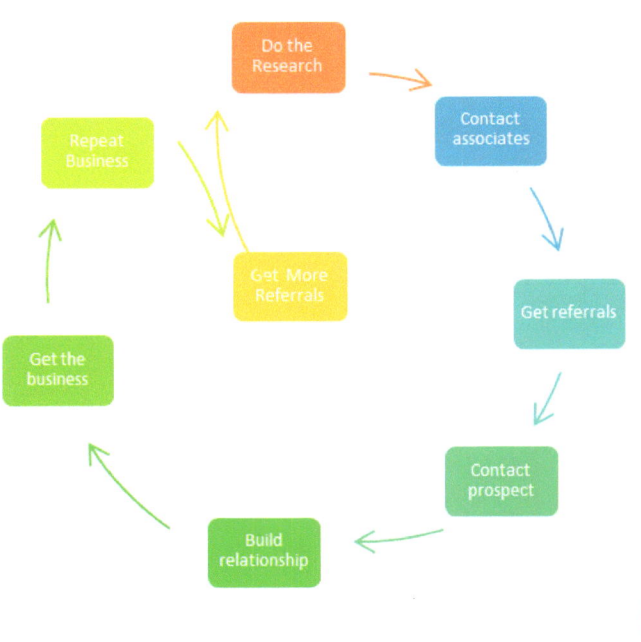

This is your engine that drives your business on the road to Success land.

You must keep this marketing engine running smoothly; by injecting it with new contacts, referrals and customers.

Create a budget for your marketing engine. You have three types of currency you can spend in this budget. These are the tools with you will make adjustments and fine tool the running of the marketing engine.

Time, Attention and Money
(Spend and use them wisely)

As you find tools, much like this book you will fine-tune your skills and continue to develop a mastery of small business ownership. If you want your marketing plan to be effective you must apply your time and attention to it.

Using Time Wisely

One method of increasing your efficiency in the area of research is to use the internet for the research engine that it is. Learn how to do key-word searches like:

Administrators buyer janitorial services contact 312 list.

(zipcodes are equally effective)

This will give you the results of anyone listed on the internet as an administrator who is related who buys janitorial services and has a contact phone number which includes 312 as the area code and if they are on a list.

In some cases, I have the entire list of people. Make sure to copy and save the information in an excel spreadsheet or word document for future use.

Keep in mind that some of these steps

require more than one day's worth of work.

so

Don't forget to allocate your time, just as you allocate your money.

Business Schedule	Marketing Schedule						
	Mon	Tue	Wed	Thurs	Fri	Sat	Sun
6 am- 8 am							
Morning							
Lunch							
Afternoon							
Evening/After Work(regular job							
After Dinner							

Make mini-plans which determine what pieces of the marketing pie you eat each day.

You will focus your time, attention and money to then create a schedule of what activities.

If you create a schedule to divide and focus your time consistently; you will see results.

STEP NINE

Create a priority list of first contacts, second contacts and third contacts. Place these contacts on your daily schedule. If you use a calendar such as Outlook or Google calendar, include reminders to ensure that you are following up and following through with your assigned tasks.

If you are using a calling list for first contact; Create and practice a script so that you don't sound nervous or confused when calling on clients.

Calling scripts can be a simple as: Hello, may I speak to Mr. Smith or as intricate as you need them to be. Remember you only purpose for calling is to

Either schedule a meeting or qualify a contact.

Think of it as speaking to the person face to face. Tell the how the benefit of your product or service.

Keeping in mind what is your goal.

Make an appointment where you can sell yourself:

People buy from people who they like and they will refer their friend, family, neighbors and associates to people who they like and trust.

Next, remember to ask for the boss. Don't be afraid, it is one president of a company speaking to another president of a company. You are on a level playing field. Even if it your piece of land is smaller than his. Remember calling on off-hours sometimes gives you a chance to reach them before they get too busy.

But be respectful: if they came in early its' probably because they are busy.

If you send a letter in advance of your call, you can use the letter as the reason for the call i.e. to review the information that you sent.

STEP TEN

Create a follow through plan so that you can measure how effective your marketing engine is running. Record all out-going and incoming calls. If you receive referrals from clients or prospects;
follow-through immediately and send a letter of thank you to your client or contact.

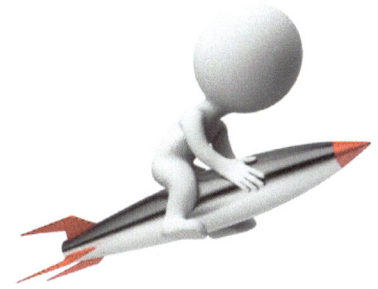

Referrals are like rocket fuel to the marketing engine; the more you get the faster and farther you can go on the road to success.

Follow through is critical on the tasks of the Marketing and Selling Cycle:

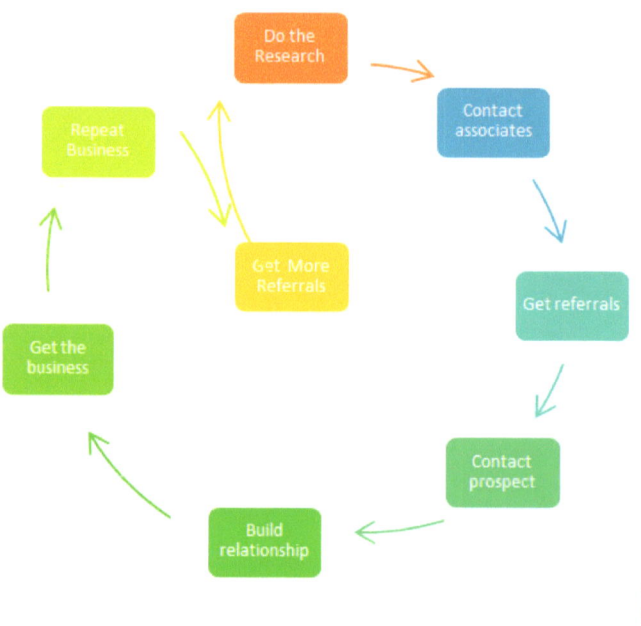

Be measureable. Check to see which methods of marketing are more effective. Which of your clients consistently provide you with referrals and at what time are you most effective at making calls that result in appointments, referrals and business?

STEP ELEVEN

Step outside and visit your best prospects.

Stop by their offices to ensure that things are running smoothly. Developing rapport through great customer service is the gas that fuels the marketing engine. And though Customer Service is not listed as a part of the Marketing Pie without great customer service you spin you wheels never going forward.

STEP TWELVE

Look at your business plan again.

Refine it. How close are you to your three month goal.

What areas can you adjust, refine or remove. Repeat the cycle and watch as you fast track down the road to success.

STAY THE COURSE:

THE ROAD MAY GET BUMPY AND CURVY,

BUT NEVER GIVE, NEVER GIVE UP AND YOU WILL REACH YOUR DESTINATION.

Forms and Appendices

Sole Proprietorships

The vast majority of small businesses start out as sole proprietorships. These firms are owned by one person, usually the individual who has day-to-day responsibilities for running the business. Sole proprietors own all the assets of the business and the profits generated by it. They also assume complete responsibility for any of its
liabilities or debts. In the eyes of the law and the public, you are one in the same with the business.

Advantages of a Sole Proprietorship:

- Easiest and least expensive form of ownership to organize.
- Sole proprietors are in complete control, and within the parameters of the law, may make decisions as they see fit.
- Sole proprietors receive all income generated by the business to keep or reinvest.
- Profits from the business flow directly to the owner's personal tax return.
- The business is easy to dissolve, if desired.

Disadvantages of a Sole Proprietorship:
- Sole proprietors have unlimited liability and are legally responsible for all debts against the

  business. Their business and personal assets are at risk.
- May be at a disadvantage in raising funds and are often limited to using funds from personal savings or consumer loans.
- May have a hard time attracting high-caliber employees or those that are motivated by the opportunity to own a part of the business.
- Some employee benefits such as owner's medical insurance premiums are not directly deductible from business income (only partially deductible as an adjustment to income).

Federal Tax Forms for Sole Proprietorship:
(only a partial list and some may not apply)
- Form 1040: Individual Income Tax Return

- Schedule C: Profit or Loss from Business (or Schedule C-EZ)
- Schedule SE: Self-Employment Tax
- Form 1040-ES: Estimated Tax for Individuals
- Form 4562: Depreciation and Amortization
- Form 8829: Expenses for Business Use of your Home
- Employment Tax Forms

Partnerships

In a Partnership, two or more people share ownership of a single business. Like proprietorships, the law does not distinguish between the business and its owners. The partners should have a legal agreement that sets forth how decisions will be made, profits will be shared, disputes will be resolved, how future partners will be admitted to the partnership, how partners can be bought out, and what steps will be taken to dissolve the partnership when needed. Yes, it's hard to think about a breakup when the business is just getting started, but many partnerships
split up at crisis times, and unless there is a defined process, there will be even greater problems. They also must decide up-front how much time and capital each will contribute, etc.

Advantages of a Partnership:

- Partnerships are relatively easy to establish; however time should be invested
in developing the partnership agreement.
- With more than one owner, the ability to raise funds may be increased.
- The profits from the business flow directly through to the partners' personal
tax returns.
- Prospective employees may be attracted to the business if given the incentive
to become a partner.
- The business usually will benefit from partners who have complementary skills.

Disadvantages of a Partnership:

- Partners are jointly and individually liable for the actions of the other partners.
- Profits must be shared with others.
- Since decisions are shared, disagreements can occur.
- Some employee benefits are not deductible from business income on tax returns.
6. The partnership may have a limited life; it may end upon the withdrawal or death of a partner.

Types of Partnerships that should be considered (these are meant as explanation not advisory- please contact your experts!)

1. General Partnership
Partners divide responsibility for management and liability as well as the shares of
profit or loss according to their internal agreement. Equal shares are assumed
unless there is a written agreement that states differently.

2. Limited Partnership and Partnership with limited liability.

Limited means that most of the partners have limited liability (to the extent of their
investment) as well as limited input regarding management decisions, which
generally encourages investors for short-term projects or for investing in capital
assets. This form of ownership is not often used for operating retail or service
businesses. Forming a limited partnership is more complex and formal than that of a
general partnership.

3. Joint Venture

Acts like a general partnership, but is clearly for a limited period of time or a single project. If the partners in a joint venture repeat the activity, they will be recognized as an ongoing partnership and will have to file as such as well as distribute accumulated partnership assets upon dissolution of the entity.

Federal Tax Forms for Partnerships:
(only a partial list and some may not apply)

- Form 1065: Partnership Return of Income
- Form 1065 K-1: Partner's Share of Income, Credit, Deductions
- Form 4562: Depreciation
- Form 1040: Individual Income Tax Return
- Schedule E: Supplemental Income and Loss
- Schedule SE: Self-Employment Tax
- Form 1040-ES: Estimated Tax for Individuals
- Employment Tax Forms

Corporations

A corporation chartered by the state in which it is headquartered is considered by law to be a unique entity, separate and apart from those who own it. A corporation can be taxed, it can be sued, and it can enter into contractual agreements. The owners of a corporation are its shareholders. The shareholders elect a board of directors to oversee the major policies and decisions. The corporation has a life of its own and does not dissolve when ownership changes.

Advantages of a Corporation:

- Shareholders have limited liability for the corporation's debts or judgments against the corporations.
- Generally, shareholders can only be held accountable for their investment in stock of the company. (Note however, that officers can be held personally liable for their actions, such as the failure to withhold and pay employment taxes.)
- Corporations can raise additional funds through the sale of stock.

- A corporation may deduct the cost of benefits it provides to officers and employees.
- Can elect S corporation status if certain requirements are met. This election enables company to be taxed similar to a partnership.

Disadvantages of a Corporation:

- The process of incorporation requires more time and money than other forms of organization.
- Corporations are monitored by federal, state and some local agencies, and as a result may have more paperwork to comply with regulations.
- Incorporating may result in higher overall taxes. Dividends paid to shareholders are not deductible from business income; thus it can be taxed twice.

Federal Tax Forms for Regular or "C" Corporations (only a partial list and some may not apply)

- Form 1120 or 1120-A: Corporation Income Tax Return
- Form 1120-W Estimated Tax for Corporation
- Form 8109-B Deposit Coupon
- Form 4625 Depreciation
- Employment Tax Forms
- Other forms as needed for capital gains, sale of assets, alternative minimum tax, etc.

Subchapter S Corporations
A tax election only; this election enables the shareholder to treat the earnings and profits as distributions and have them pass through directly to their personal tax return. The catch here is that the shareholder, if working for the company, and if there is a profit, must pay him/herself wages, and must meet standards of "reasonable compensation". This can vary by geographical region as well as occupation, but the basic rule is to pay yourself what you would have to pay someone to do your job, as long as

there is enough profit. If you do not do this, the IRS can reclassify all of the earnings and profit as wages, and you will be liable for all of the payroll taxes on the total amount.

Federal Tax Forms for Subchapter S Corporations: (only a partial list and some may not apply)

- Form 1120S: Income Tax Return for S Corporation
- 1120S K-1: Shareholder's Share of Income, Credit, Deductions
- Form 4625 Depreciation
- Employment Tax Forms
- Form 1040: Individual Income Tax Return
- Schedule E: Supplemental Income and Loss
- Schedule SE: Self-Employment Tax
- Form 1040-ES: Estimated Tax for Individuals
- Other forms as needed for capital gains, sale of assets, alternative minimum tax, etc.

Limited Liability Company (LLC)
The LLC is a relatively new type of hybrid business structure that is now permissible in most states. It is designed to provide the limited liability features of a corporation and the tax efficiencies and operational flexibility of a partnership. Formation is more complex and formal than that of a general partnership.
The owners are members, and the duration of the LLC is usually determined when the organization papers are filed. The time limit can be continued, if desired, by a vote of the members at the time of expiration. LLCs must not have more than two of the four characteristics that define corporations: Limited liability to the extent of assets,
continuity of life, centralization of management, and free transferability of ownership interests.
Federal Tax Forms for LLC:
Taxed as partnership in most cases; corporation forms must be used if there are more than 2 of
the 4 corporate characteristics, as described above.
In summary, deciding the form of ownership that best suits your business venture should be given careful consideration.

Use your expert advisers to assist you in the process.
Don't be a know it all
(supplied courtesy of the Small Business Administration)

BUSINESS PLAN OUTLINE

Cover Sheet: Name(s) of principles(s); name, address and phone # of business.

STATEMENT OF PURPOSE

TABLE OF CONTENTS

I. THE BUSINESS

    A. Description of the Business

    B. The Market

    C. Competition and Feasibility Study

    D. Location of Business

    E. Management

    F. Personnel

    G. Application and Expected Effect of Loan or Investment

    H. Summary

II. FINANCIAL DATA

    A. Sources and Application of Funding

    B. Capital Equipment and Furniture Lists

    C. Projected Balance Sheet

    D. Break-even Analysis

    E. Projected Income Statements

        * Three-year Summary

        * Detail by Month, First Year

        * Detail by Quarter, Second and Third Years

        * Notes of Explanation

    F. Cash Flow Projections

        * Three-year Summary

        * Detail by Month, First Year

        * Detail by Quarter, Second and Third Years

        * Notes of Explanation

    G. For an Existing Business (also include the following documents)

        * Profit/Loss Statements for Past Three Years

* Balance Sheets for Past Three Years
* Business Income Tax Returns for past Three Years
* Personal Income Tax Returns for Past Three Years

III. SUPPORTING DOCUMENTS

Personal resume, job descriptions, personal financial statements, credit reports, letter of reference, letters of intent, leases, contracts, other legal documents, and anything else of relevance to the plan.

STATEMENT OF PURPOSE

A brief (less than 1 page) statement of the business plan objectives.

QUESTIONS – to consider

In General:

1. What is the purpose of this plan?

Will it be used as an:

- operating guide?
- financing proposal

2. What is the business structure (i.e., sole proprietorship, general partnership, limited partnership, C corporation, or Subchapter S corporation
3. Who is (are) the principle(s)?
4. What is to be done?
5. Why will it be successful? For A Financing Proposal:
6. Who is asking for money?
7. How much money is being requested?
8. What is the money needed for?
9. How will the funds benefit the business?
10. How will the funds be repaid?
11. Why does the loan or investment make sense?

A. DESCRIPTION OF THE BUSINESS

GENERALLY EXPLAIN:

1. What the business is (or will be):

2. What market you intend to service, the size of the market, and your expected share;

3. Why you can service what market better than your competition;

4. Why you have chosen your particular location;

5. What management and other personnel are required and available for the operation; and

6. Why your investment or someone else's money (debt/equity) will help make your business profitable.

QUESTIONS:

1. Type of business; <u>primarily</u> merchandising retail, manufacturing, wholesale, or service?

2. What is the nature of the product(s) or service(s)?

3. Status of business start-up, expansion of a going concern, or take-over of an existing business?

4. Business form: sole proprietorship, partnership or corporation?

5. Who are the customers or clients?

6. Why is your business going to be profitable?

7. When will (did) your business open?

8. What hours of the day and days of the week will you be (are you) in operation?

9. What have you learned about your kind of business from outside sources (trade suppliers, banks, other business people, publications)?

NOTE: If yours is a seasonal business, or if the hours will be adjusted seasonally, make sure that the seasonality is reflected in your replies to the two previous questions.

FOR A NEW BUSINESS

10. Why will you be successful in this business?

11. What is <u>your</u> experience in this business?

12. Have you spoken with other people in this type of business about their experience, challenges and rewards? What were their responses?

13. What will be special about your business?

14. Have you spoken with prospective trade suppliers to find out what managerial and/or technical help they will provide?

15. Have you asked about trade credit?

16. If you will be doing and contract work, what are the terms? Reference any firm contract and include it as a supporting document.

17. Do you have letters of intent from prospective suppliers or purchasers?

FOR A TAKE-OVER:

18. When and by whom was the business founded?

19. Why is the owner selling it?

20. How did you arrive at a purchase price for the business?

21. What is the trend of sales?

22. If the business is going downhill, why? How can you turn it around?

23. How will your management make the business more profitable?

B. THE MARKET
Generally explain who needs your product or service, and why.

QUESTIONS:
1. Who exactly is your market? Describe characteristics: age, sex, profession, income, etc., of your various market segments.

2. What is the present size of the market?

3. What percent of the market will you have?

4. What is the market's growth potential?

5. As the market grows, will your share increase of decrease?

6. How are you going to satisfy the market?

7. How will you attract and keep your share of the market?

8. How can you expand your market?

9. How are you going to price your service or product, to make a fair profit, and at the same time, be competitive?

10. What price do you anticipate getting for your product or service?

11. Is the price competitive?

12. Why will someone pay you price?

13. How did you arrive at the price? Is it profitable?

14. What special advantage do you offer that may justify a higher price? (You don't necessarily have to engage in direct price competition).

15. Will you offer credit to your customers (accounts receivable)? If so, is this really necessary? Can you afford to extend credit? Can you afford bad debts?

C. COMPETITION QUESTIONS:

1. Who are your five nearest competitors? List them by name.

2. How will your operation be better than theirs?

3. How is their business: steady? increasing? decreasing? Why?

4. How are their operations similar and dissimilar to yours?

5. What are their strengths and/or weaknesses?

6. What have you learned from watching their operations?

7. How do you plan to keep an eye on the competition in the future?

D. LOCATION OF BUSINESS

1. What kind of building do you need?

2. What are the attributes and/or salient features of your present or desired business location?

3. Why is this a desirable area?

4. Why is this a desirable building?

5. Does the community around which you intend to locate the business show enthusiasm for you and your business?

6. What are the advantages and disadvantages of the site in terms of wage rates, labor unions, and labor availability?

7. How much space do you need?

8. Do you need a long-term or short-term lease?

9. Is the building accessible by public transportation?

10. Is the building close to customers or suppliers?

11. Is free or low cost parking nearby?

12. What are the state and local taxes, laws, utilities, zoning, and variables that may affect the location of you business?
13 How do you plan to keep an eye on any demographic shift in your area?

E. MANAGEMENT QUESTIONS:
1. What is your business background?
2. How does your background/business experience help you in this business?
3. What management experience do you have?
4. Do you have managerial experience in this type of business?
5. Do you have managerial experience acquired elsewhere-whether in totally different kinds of business, or as an offshoot of club or team membership, civic or church work, etc.?
6. What weakness do you have and how will you compensate for them, i.e., will you hire employees or pay consultants who have management abilities/expertise that you don't have?
7. What education do you have (including both formal and informal learning experience) which have bearing on your managerial abilities or knowledge of the industry?
8. Personal data: age; where you live and have lived; special abilities and interests; and reasons for going into business?
9. Are you physically suited to the job? Stamina counts.
10. Why are you going to be successful at this venture?
11. Do you have direct operational experience in this type of business?
12. Who is on the management team?
13. What are the duties of each individual on the management team?
14. Are these duties clearly defined? how?
15. Who does what? Who reports to whom? Where do final decisions get made?
16. What and how will management be paid?
17. What additional resources have you arranged to have available to help you and your business
(accountant, lawyer, et al.).

NOTE: A personal financial statement must be included as a supporting document in your plan if it is a proposal for financing. Also, include your resume as a supporting document.

F. **PERSONNEL QUESTIONS**:

1. What are your personnel needs now? In the near future (3years)? In five years?

2. What skills must they have?

3. Are the people you need available?

4. Will your employees be full-time or part-time?

5. Will you pay salaries or hourly wages?

6. Certain employee benefits are mandatory. Find out what they are.

7. Will you provide additional fringe benefits? If so, which ones? Have you calculated the cost of these additional fringe benefits?

8. Will you utilize overtime? If so, you may be required by law to pay time and a half, double time, and/or other extra costs.

9. Will you have to train people for both operations and management? If so, at what costs to the business?

Bibliography

Crandall, Rick. *Marketing You Services: For People Who Hate to Sell.* Chicago: Contemporary Books, 1996.

Knight, Sue. *NLP at Work: The Difference that makes a difference in business.* Naperville IL: Nicholas Brealey Publishing Limited, 1999.

Lambert, Tom. *High Income Consulting.* Naperville IL: Nicholas Brealey Publishing Limited, 1999.

Salmon, Bil, and Nate Rosenblan. *The Complete Book of Consulting.* Ridgefield, CT: Round Lake Publishing Co., 1995.

www.ingramcontent.com/pod-product-compliance
Lightning Source LLC
Chambersburg PA
CBHW040834180526
45159CB00001B/185